HIRAM HALLE MEMORIAL LIBRARY
271 Westchester Avenue
Pound Ridge, New York
10576-1714

5/98 B+T

Trevor's Story

Bethany Kandel
Photographs by Carol Halebian

⌐ LERNER PUBLICATIONS COMPANY / MINNEAPOLIS

J
306.84
K

To my family for their unfailing love and support,
and to the Sage-EL family for welcoming me into
their home and hearts.

— Bethany Kandel

Illustrations by John Erste

Copyright © 1997 by Bethany Kandel

All rights reserved. International copyright secured. No part of this book
may be reproduced or transmitted in any form or by any means, electronic
or mechanical, including photocopying and recording, or by any
information storage or retrieval system, without permission in writing from
Lerner Publications Company, except for the inclusion of brief quotations
in an acknowledged review.

LIBRARY OF CONGRESS CATALOGING-IN-PUBLICATION DATA

Kandel, Bethany.
    Trevor's story : growing up biracial / Bethany Kandel ;
photographs by Carol Halebian.
        p. cm.
    Includes bibliographical references.
    Summary: Ten-year-old Trevor Sage-EL describes his life at home
and at school, his feelings about being the son of a white mother and a
black father, and what he likes and does not like about being biracial.
    ISBN 0-8225-2583-6 (alk. paper)
    1. Children of interracial marriage—Juvenile literature.
2. Interracial marriage—Juvenile literature. [1. Interracial marriage.
2. Racially mixed people. 3. Identity.] I. Halebian, Carol, ill. II. Title.
HQ777.9.K36 1997
306.84'6—DC21   96-44523

Manufactured in the United States of America
1 2 3 4 5 6 – JR – 02 01 00 99 98 97

AUTHOR'S NOTE

When I was growing up, the traditional family, especially the families I saw on television, had a mother, father, and two or three children who all looked basically alike. But that family is no longer the norm. Families are often made up of people of different cultures, races, religions, and colors. In a country that segregated the races as recently as the 1960s—with laws that required black people in the South to drink from different water fountains than whites, attend separate schools, and sit in the back of the bus—a biracial family was once unusual. But biracial and multiracial families are more and more common in the United States.

Despite the increase in the number of biracial and multiracial children in America, they continue to encounter discrimination and negative reactions. Many multiracial people hope to convince local and federal governments to create a "multiracial" category on official forms that ask people to indicate their race. That way people like Trevor won't be forced to list themselves as "other" when they don't fit the existing categories such as black, white, Asian, or Native American.

Trevor's story shows some of the joys and problems of being biracial, yet his story is unique. Every biracial or multiracial child has a different experience.

Many parents and teachers want children to embrace diversity and appreciate one another's differences as well as their similarities. My hope is that by reading Trevor's story, kids will realize that people of different races do not have to hate one another.

As Trevor will tell you, "There really is only one race—the human race."

Bethany Kandel

CONTENTS

Trevor's Story / 7

Information about Biracial Children
and Families / 34

Glossary / 36

Resources / 38

For Further Reading / 40

ONCE IN A WHILE someone asks me, "What are you?" I usually answer, "Human." When one kid at school asked me, that's what I said. Then I asked him, "What are *you?* Alien?" I've always wondered, why do I have to *be* anything? We're all part of the human race. So far as I know, no one has proven that aliens exist.

My name is Trevor Mark Sage-EL. I am ten years old and I am biracial. My mom, Margot, is white. My dad, Barry, is black. I am kind of a light tan color.

Sometimes people ask me if I'm adopted. They can't believe that my mom is my mom. Some people even think she's my babysitter! I guess my family and I are not what people are used to. Some of my friends, even though they're teenagers, still don't get it.

The other day my friend Sam asked me why my mother is white, my father is black, and I'm brown. I told him that when two people who are different colors, like black and white, have a baby, the child is a mix of both colors—light brown or tan, sort of like the color of a brown paper bag.

It's not like mixing paint. Another kid in my class asked me why I'm not gray, because when he mixes black and white paint he ends up with gray.

If you look closely at people, you see that they are not really black or white. White people are more of a pale peach or pink or beige, unless they're very frightened and they're as white as a ghost. And black people are different shades of brown, from dark coffee to light toast.

If I had to describe myself, I'd say that I'm the color of chocolate milk. My dad is the color of Hershey's syrup. My mom jokes that she's the milk! But she's really more the color of an unpainted canvas.

I'M IN FIFTH GRADE at Northeast International School in Montclair, New Jersey. My favorite subjects are science and reading. I do well in school, except for math, especially division. I didn't remember the steps to figure out the problems, so it was really hard. But now I have a tutor, Jane, who teaches me little tricks. She says she's going to make a math whiz out of me. Before she came, I got a very low grade on my division test. But after she practiced with me, I got a 92!

I'm on the wrestling team at school and I play baseball. Last year I played outfield. That position was kind of boring because not many balls came out there—and when they did, I was already asleep and I missed them. Right now I'm the pitcher on my team, the Mets. But I don't like the real Major League Mets team because they're doing terribly. I like the Yankees. They're doing a lot better.

My nickname is "Bean" because I'm skinny like a string bean. I eat a lot but I still only weigh 60 pounds. My parents want me to gain more weight, so they're always asking my wrestling coach for advice on how to fatten me up.

My favorite food is macaroni and cheese. I love the way my mom makes it. My friend Andrew complains that his mom can't make macaroni and cheese, so my mom gave her the recipe. (There's no big secret, she says, just basic elbow pasta and cheddar cheese.) Another of my friends, Kevin, also loves macaroni and cheese. He comes over for supper sometimes.

I have two sisters—Madeleine, who's nine, and Olivia, who's four. Sometimes Maddie and I fight, but then the next minute we're best friends. My sisters like me to play Barbie dolls with them. I'll only do it when they're really nice to me. I always have to be Ken and play the boyfriend or the father.

I'd rather go in-line skating or snowboarding or play paintball with my friends. In paintball, we split up into two teams and fill our Super Soaker water guns with red and blue dyed water. Then we go around the neighborhood and try to hunt each other down and squirt each other. Whoever gets soaked by the opposite team is out.

When I grow up I want to be in the FBI. My friends call me "Top Gun" because I'm the best at paintball. I'm fast and I can shoot real far. Plus, I'm sneaky. The only person I can't sneak up on is my dad.

My bedroom is on the top floor of our house. I sleep there all by myself. It can be a little creepy at night. My cat Alvin (named after Alvin and the Chipmunks) sleeps with me, but I get annoyed with him in the middle of the night. He walks all over me and lies on my legs. Then I have to push him off.

My mom is always yelling at me to clean my room. I did it yesterday ... but you can't really tell. When Maddie and I don't listen to our parents, they send us to our rooms. I have a TV up there, a computer, my comics, and trading cards, so it's not so bad.

My dad is a computer programmer. My mom just bought a bookstore in our town. I love to help her at the cash register. Last week I checked a whole order that came in to make sure the right number of books and the correct titles were all there.

My mom also has a catalog company that sells multicultural books and books about biracial families. She started it because she couldn't find any books to read to me and my sisters about families like ours.

WHEN I WAS LITTLE I didn't know I was biracial. I used to think that I was just really suntanned. I wondered why my parents weren't tan like me. But I thought it was normal not to look like your parents. I have a good friend, Moses, whose dad is Japanese and whose mom is white. He doesn't really look like either of them.

18

I found out by myself that I was biracial. My parents were talking to somebody and I heard them say the word and heard my name after it. I didn't know what it meant. The next day I told my friend that I was biracial. He said, "What's that?" I didn't know. Eventually I understood what it meant—that I'm a mix of two colors or races.

Since then, I've learned that there are lots of words used to describe me, like *multiracial* and *interracial.* People used to call children with one white and one black parent *mulattos.* But that word is outdated.

My parents talk to me about what it means to be biracial and how to deal with racism—when someone picks on me just because of the color of my skin. My mom and dad tell me that if someone says something insulting to me, I should just walk away from them. That person is not educated and doesn't realize that people of all colors are equal.

Even though I would like to handle those situations by fighting, I know it's not right. My parents always tell me not to fight because they don't believe in violence. They also don't want people to have a bad impression of me. They say I can find better solutions to problems.

I'M THE DARKEST OF THE KIDS in my family. My little sister Olivia is the lightest. She thinks she's white like Mom, and Maddie and I are black like our dad. When she gets older she'll understand what it means to be biracial.

In school we had to draw a self-portrait of ourselves. I drew a circle and put a face in it. Then I made a yin yang symbol out of it, half black and half white, symbolizing both parts of me. I like the yin yang symbol because one half is black and the other half is white. The yin yang represents harmony of the universe.

I know there is racism against black people—I've seen it. Things are different when I'm out with my mother than when I'm with my father. What's different is the way people treat us. One day my sisters and I were sitting at the food court in the mall with my dad, and this lady thought Dad was going to steal her purse. He was just eating a hamburger! She had a stereotype about black people—that they all steal. That wouldn't have happened if we had been there with my mom.

When my parents were applying for a mortgage for our house, they went to the bank and their application was turned down. The second time my mom went alone and the loan was approved, because the people at the bank thought that both my parents were white. That's racism and I hate it.

I admire Martin Luther King Jr., but my real hero is Jackie Robinson. He broke the color line in baseball by becoming the first African American man to play Major League baseball. It's really cool that just one person can make such a difference. Did you know that we might not have the electric light bulb, traffic lights, or blood banks if it weren't for the contributions of black people?

I LIKE IT that I have two family histories to learn about. We have a little of everything in my family: white grandparents and black grandparents; white aunts and uncles and black aunts and uncles; and cousins who are black, white, Christian, and Jewish.

Both sides of my family have experienced hate. My mother's family is from Germany. Her father was a soldier in World War II. He was drafted when he was 17 and in high school. Even though he fought with the Nazis, he wasn't a Nazi. He didn't believe in what they stood for, but he was forced to fight with them. The Nazis believed they were a superior race. Their leader, Adolf Hitler, wanted to conquer and eliminate anyone who was different. The Nazis killed millions of Jewish people in concentration camps.

In my grandparents' wedding picture, there are swastikas (the Nazi symbol) in the background, and a portrait of Hitler. That's because they got married in a German town hall. It's like the American flag hanging in a town hall here.

When the war ended, my grandfather stayed in Russia until he could escape to America. He burned his uniform. I asked him questions about the war and Hitler for a school report. My grandfather said that Hitler didn't just hate Jews, he also hated black people.

My great-great-grandmother was a slave. That makes me sad, especially because I get to do and have whatever I want, and she and her family didn't.

My father used to spend summers in Macon, Georgia, visiting his grandmother. In the South at that time, Jim Crow laws called for segregated (separate) schools, restaurants, bathrooms, and even water fountains for blacks and whites. My dad's sister, my aunt Adrienne, got in big trouble because she drank out of the "white" water fountain. She got mad because she said it was the same water. Now she's a doctor in California.

If we still had Jim Crow laws, I couldn't even drink out of the same fountain as my mother! My parents wouldn't have been able to get married and I would never have been born.

My parents met in college. My father walked into a class late one day and saw my mother sitting on the desk. He thought she was the teacher. They started dating, and they fell in love. It wasn't hard for them to decide to get married, because they loved each other—they didn't care what color they were. But their parents weren't too sure about it at first.

I might marry a biracial girl or maybe one who is black or white. I don't really know because I'm only ten years old. But I do know that I will marry somebody because of her personality—and she has to love kids.

I have friends of all colors. Andrew is white, Moses is half Japanese and half white, Sam is white, Kevin is black, and Matthew and Christopher are white. Jamie is my only close friend who's biracial. Sometimes I talk to her about things that only she can understand.

My parents are involved in a group called G.I.F.T.—
Getting Interracial/Intercultural Families Together. They
have meetings and guest speakers, and they talk about
raising biracial children. Mostly the kids just hang out, but
sometimes we have good discussions about stereotypes or we
read books.

I've never been called any names, but I've heard some of the names for biracial kids, like "Oreo" or "Zebra." (Oreo cookies and Zebras are both part black and part white.) I don't think that's very nice. I'd rather not be labeled at all.

Being half African American is part of my family's everyday life. But we also do something special during Black History Month, like going to a musical event or a play. The day after Christmas, we also light candles for Kwanzaa either at our house or at our friends'.

IT'S NO PROBLEM BEING BIRACIAL in our town, because it's very mixed. A black family lives next door; on the other side is a white family; down the block it's black, white, black, white.

I also go to an international school where kids come from all over the world, including Russia, Africa, Germany, and Puerto Rico. We have many different flags hanging up and we have exhibits and plays about different countries.

I know that some biracial kids are the only ones in their town. People may not like them because of the color of their skin. If they asked me for advice, I would tell them to keep their distance from people who are racist.

Stand up for yourself, but be careful what you say. You don't want to push someone's button and make that person mad. Being angry or making someone else angry won't solve any problems. Some people just won't change.

The hard thing about being biracial is that you may get teased and you may be asked to choose between being black or being white. I don't want to choose. One of my parents is black and one is white, so I'm both.

There are positives, too. I'm probably less prejudiced than a lot of other kids. I don't make fun of people or judge them because of their differences.

Sometimes I wish my parents were the same color, but then I realize that if I was one color I wouldn't be able to tell people what it's like to be biracial. Maybe I have taught other kids to be more tolerant and accepting of differences.

If everybody was biracial or multiracial it would be a lot better. Everyone would understand that it doesn't matter what color you are, it just matters what kind of person you are. It's what's on the inside that counts.

Information about
BIRACIAL CHILDREN AND FAMILIES

About two million children in the United States have parents of different races. The number of children born to parents of different races has been steadily climbing: they made up 4.1 percent of all U.S. births in 1993, compared to only 1.5 percent of births in 1973. And this is probably an underestimate.

The number of interracial marriages (marriages between people of different races) in the United States continues to rise, from 321,000 in 1970 to more than 1.4 million in 1990. While marrying someone of a different color may seem common, not too long ago it was against the law. Most states banned interracial marriage at some point in their history. It wasn't until 1967 that the United States Supreme Court overturned the last such laws.

Despite legal changes, children of biracial and multiracial relationships still face challenges. Some biracial children identify themselves as one color or the other. But many embrace their entire racial heritage. They choose to identify themselves as biracial or multiracial.

They and their parents are behind a movement to change the way official forms ask people to classify themselves by race. Most government, school, and employment forms and applications don't list "multiracial" as a category, so people who fit that description usually check the box marked "other" to indicate their race. Many people hope to create a "multiracial" category to acknowledge the background of people who don't fit the existing racial categories.

Laws have already been passed in five states (Georgia, Illinois, Indiana, Ohio, and Michigan) to add a multiracial category on various official forms. Two other states (Florida and North Carolina) have added the category on all school forms. Many other states are considering such changes, and the federal government has been studying whether to add a multiracial classification on the 2000 census.

(Sources: the 1990 Census, the National Center for Health Statistics)

GLOSSARY

biracial—(BYE-ray-shull)—involving or combining two races

color—a person's complexion or skin tone; the term is also used to refer to race

discrimination—(dis-CRIM-ih-NAY-shun)—unfair treatment based on something such as race or disability

diversity—(dih-VER-sih-tee)—difference or variety

FBI—abbreviation for the Federal Bureau of Investigation; the investigating branch of the United States government

intermarriage—marriage between two people of different races, religions, or ethnic groups

interracial—involving members of different races

Jim Crow laws—required separation of the races in many public places in the Southern United States, including schools, restaurants, theaters, restrooms, and water fountains. Signs often labeled these places "white" and "colored." The laws were declared invalid in the 1950s and 1960s.

Kwanzaa—an African American holiday that starts on December 26 and lasts six days. Each day a candle is lit and one of the seven principles of Kwanzaa is remembered: unity, self-determination, collective work and responsibility, cooperative economics, purpose, creativity, and faith.

mortgage—(MORE-guhj)—an agreement by which someone borrows money to buy a house. If the borrower does not pay back the loan, the lender (often a bank) can take ownership of the property.

multicultural—involving many different backgrounds and cultures

multiracial—having parents of different races or being in a family where at least two of the people are of a different race

Nazi—a member of the National Socialist German Workers' Party, founded in Germany in 1919 and brought to power in 1933 under dictator Adolf Hitler. Nazis glorified Germans and other Northern European people and claimed that Jews, blacks, and other minority groups were inferior.

prejudice—(PREH-juh-dis)—an unfavorable opinion, feeling, or attitude directed against a racial, religious, or national group; an opinion formed without knowledge, thought, or reason

race—a large segment of the population with common physical characteristics, including skin color, shape of eyes, and stature, though some members may differ widely in features

racism—(RAY-sih-zum)—the practice of racial discrimination based on the belief that one race is superior to another

segregate—(SEG-gruh-gate)—to require the separation of a racial, religious, or other subgroup from the main group

stereotype—(STARE-ee-oh-type)—the belief that a person or members of a group conform to an unvarying pattern or manner, without individuality

tolerant—(TALL-ur-uhnt)—inclined to recognize and respect others' beliefs, practices, and values, without necessarily agreeing or sympathizing

yin yang—a Chinese symbol in which one half of a circle is white or red and the other is black, representing the harmony of the universe

Resources

A Place For Us Ministry for Interracial Couples
P.O. Box 357
Gardena, CA 90248-7857
(213) 779-1717
(Multiracial family support organization)

Association of MultiEthnic Americans
P.O. Box 191726
San Francisco, CA 94119-1726
E-mail: AMEAPRES@aol.com
(773) 288-7390
(408) 297-6277

Interrace Publications
P.O. Box 12048
Atlanta, GA 30355
(404) 350-7877
(Publishers of *Child of Colors* and *Interrace* magazines)

Portraits of Multiracial Families
c/o Peggy Gillespie
P.O. Box 1209
Amherst, MA 01004-1209
(413) 256-0502.
(A photograph-text exhibit)

Project RACE
1425 Market Boulevard
Suite 1320-E6
Roswell, GA 30076
(770) 433-6076
(Working to expand the use of the "multiracial" classification
on official forms)

Sources for biracial and multiracial books:

Great Owl Books
33 Watchung Plaza
Montclair, NJ 07042
(201) 744-7177
(800) 299-3181

Highsmith Inc.
W5527 Highway 106
P.O. Box 800
Fort Atkinson, WI 53538-0800
(800) 558-2110

For Further **READING**

For children

Brady, April A. *Kwanzaa Karamu: Cooking and Crafts for a Kwanzaa Feast.* Minneapolis: Carolrhoda Books, 1995.

Davol, Marguerite. *Black, White, Just Right.* Morton Grove, Illinois: Albert Whitman, 1993.

Mandelbaum, Pili. *You Be Me/I'll Be You.* New York: Kane/Miller Book Publishers, 1990.

Pellegrini, Nina. *Families are Different.* New York: Holiday House, 1991.

Porter, A.P. *Kwanzaa.* Minneapolis: Carolrhoda Books, 1991.

Wyeth, Sharon. *The World of Daughter McGuire.* New York: Delacorte Press, 1994.

For adults

Funderburg, Lise. *Black, White, Other.* New York: Morrow, 1994.

Mathabane, Mark and Gail. *Love in Black and White.* New York: Harper Collins, 1992.

Reddy, Maureen. *Crossing the Color Line.* New Brunswick, N.J.: Rutgers University Press, 1994.

HIRAM HALLE MEM (POUND RIDGE)

3 1026 10039594 4

J

306.84   Kandel, Bethany.
K   Trevor's story.

Hiram Halle Memorial Library
Pound Ridge, New York

GAYLORD